Some people dream of worthy accomplishments, while others stay awake and do them.

Compiled by Peg Anderson

ISBN: 1-880461-24-2

Printed in the U.S.A.

G O A L S

Goals are funny things. They don't work unless you do.

Goals without time limits are only wishes.

Dare mighty things, even though checkered with failure, rather than to rank with those grey souls that know neither victory or defeat.

– THEODORE ROOSEVELT

Many people have a good aim in life, but for some reason they never pull the trigger.

G O A L S

Goals are like automobiles, they won't run by themselves except downhill.

The secret of success is constancy to purpose.

– BENJAMIN DISRAELI

G O A L S

To achieve happiness, we should make certain that we are never without an important goal.

– EARL NIGHTINGALE

G O A L S

If you don't know where you're going, you may miss it when you get there.

G O A L S

Before following a leader it is wise to see if he is headed in the right direction.

Your life can't go according to plan if you have no plan.

Some people would rather look backward than forward because it's easier to remember where you've been than to figure out where you're going.

It is not enough to make progress; we must make it in the right direction.

Keep your head and your heart going in the right direction and you'll not have to worry about your feet.

A goal to be the best is more important than a goal to be the biggest.

What would you try to accomplish if you believed it was impossible to fail?

In great attempts it is glorious to fail.

– CASSIUS

Not failure, but low aim, is a crime.

— JAMES RUSSELL LOWELL

Great minds have purposes, others have wishes.

– WASHINGTON IRVING

G O A L S

The good man is the man who, no matter how morally unworthy he has been, is moving to become better.

– JOHN DEWEY

Failure is not necessarily missing the target, but aiming too low.

*Do not simply be good-
be good for something.*

G O A L S

Goals are not only absolutely necessary to motivate us. They are essential to really keep us alive.

– ROBERT H. SCHULLER

G O A L S

The world makes way for the man who knows where he is going.

– RALPH W. EMERSON

The reason most people in business flounder is that they are without goals.

Many a person who started out to conquer the world in shining armor has ended up just getting along. The horse got tired, the armor rusty. The goal was removed and unsure.

– ROBERT A. COOK

A person going nowhere can be sure of reaching his destination.

The greatest danger for most of us is not that our aim is too high and we miss it, but that our aim is too low and we reach it.

Our aim should be service, not success.

When you determine what you want, you have made the most important decision in your life. You have to know what you want in order to attain it.

– DOUGLAS LURTAN

Nothing will ever be attained if all possible objections must first be overcome.

Big goals can create a fear of failure. Lack of goals guarantees it.

Pursue worthy aims.

— SOLON

Progress has little to do with speed, but much to do with direction.

*Aim at the moon -
you'll never shoot
yourself in the foot.*

G O A L S

Set positive goals and reasonable expectations.

– STEVE STRASSER

You must have long-range goals to keep you from being frustrated by short-range failures.

— CHARLES C. NOBLE

Instead of setting goals based on outcomes, set goals which focus on performances.

Goals must be under our control. We need targets and directions upon which to focus our efforts.

Pursue one great decisive aim with force and determination.

It concerns us to know the purpose we seek in life, for then, like archers aiming at a definite mark, we shall be more likely to attain what we want.

— ARISTOTLE

Shared goals build unity.

Goal "setting" is important...Goal "doing" is <u>more</u> important.

Goals help to define our uniqueness.

Goals create focus.

Goals and action must meet.

Big goals require the accomplishment of many little goals.

Expect to accomplish what you attempt.

Goals give direction, purpose, and meaning to life.

Great goals require great passion.

It may be a long way to a goal, but it is never far to the next step towards your goal.

Enjoy the pursuit of your goals.

Action speaks louder than words.

G O A L S

It is better to aim at a good thing and miss it than to aim at a bad thing and hit it.

Success is determined by goals finished — not attempted.

If you are going to climb, you have to grab the branches not the blossoms.

Success comes from having the proper aim as well as the right ammunition.

Aim at the sun and you may not reach it, but your arrow will fly far higher than if aimed at an object on a level with yourself.

—JOEL HAWES

Don't sit back and take what comes...go after what you want.

Abraham Lincoln was great, not because he once lived in a cabin, but because his goals got him out of it.

There is no point in carrying the ball until you learn where the goal is.

You seldom hit anything unless you aim at it.

Management by objective gets one to look forward rather than backward.

A man with a burning ambition is seldom fired.

Make no little plans; they have no magic to stir men's souls.

G O A L S

The significance of a man is not what he attains but rather in what he longs to attain.

— KAHIL GIBRAN

The most absurd and and reckless aspirations have sometimes led to extraordinary success.

– VAUVENARGUES

GOALS

This one thing I do, forgetting those things which are behind, and reaching forth unto those things which are before, I press toward the mark!

— PHILLIPIANS 3:13

Ah, but a man's reach should exceed his grasp, or what's heaven for?

– ROBERT BROWNING

Once you say you're going to settle for second, that's what happens to you in life.

–JOHN F. KENNEDY

We never see the target a man aims at in life; we see only the target he hits.

Having the right aim in life doesn't mean a thing if you're loaded with blanks.

Goals create strength.

An achieved goal is the starting point for future progress.

G O A L S

The first two letters of goal are go...

Big goals can create a fear of failure. Lack of goals guarantees it.

G O A L S

You measure the size of the accomplishment by the obstacles you had to overcome to reach your goals.

– BOOKER T. WASHINGTON

A *goal properly set is halfway reached.*

The Success Collection

BY CELEBRATING EXCELLENCE

- Commitment to Excellence
- Management Magic
- Humourous Quotes From the Business World
- Great Quotes from Great Leaders
- Motivational Quotes
- Customer Care
- Opportunity Selling
- The Best of Success
- Commitment to Quality
- Great Quotes from Great Women
- Zig Ziglar's Favorite Quotations
- Winning With Teamwork
- The Power of Goals
- Attitude
- Pride
- Innovation & Creativity

TOLL FREE (800) 535-2773

919 Springer Drive • Lombard, IL 60148